WHAT YOU SAY TO YOUR CHILD
REALLY DOES MATTER!!!

(Starting From The Moment Of Conception To Death)!!!

LISA LEE HAIRSTON

Order this book online at www.trafford.com
or email orders@trafford.com

Most Trafford titles are also available at major online book retailers.

Scripture quotations marked KJV are from the Holy Bible, King James
Version (Authorized Version). First published in 1611. Quoted from the KJV
Classic Reference Bible, Copyright © 1983 by Zondervan Corporation.

Printed in the United States of America.

ISBN: 978-1-4907-2825-4 (sc)
ISBN: 978-1-4907-2824-7 (e)

Trafford rev. 03/10/2015

Trafford
PUBLISHING® www.trafford.com

North America & international
toll-free: 1 888 232 4444 (USA & Canada)
fax: 812 355 4082

Contents

Dedication

I dedicate this book to my 95-year-old aunt, Jessie Maud Harbor, to her mother, grandmothers, great-grandmothers, aunts, and all successive female generations. They all are the very reason this book was written—to demonstrate how to walk in Generational Blessings!!!

All Scriptures mentioned throughout this book have been taken from the Kings James and Amplified Versions of the Bible unless otherwise noted!!!

Foreword

Speak to the average person and he or she might just believe in the old adage that "opposites attract!!!" Nothing could be further from the truth!!!

Spiritual laws, beginning in the Book of Genesis, suggest that *like attracts like*!!! *"And God said, let the earth bring forth grass, the herb yielding seed, and the fruit tree yielding fruit after his kind, whose seed is in itself upon the earth, and it was so.*

And the earth brought forth grass, and herb yielding seed after his kind, and the tree yielding fruit, whose seed was in itself, after his kind, and God saw

that it was good" (Genesis 1:11-12).
The remaining verses of this chapter in Genesis continue in its mission of showing you how various things reproduce after its kind.

Similarly, love attracts love! Money attracts money! Success attracts success! Prosperity attracts prosperity! Riches attract riches! Wealth attracts wealth! Happiness attracts happiness! A happy marriage attracts a happy marriage! Living happily ever after attracts living happily ever after! And blessings attract blessings!

In this book, *What You Say To Your Child Really Does Matter: From The Moment Of Conception To Death,* you will come to understand the upmost and uttermost importance of how critical it is to begin speaking words of blessing, happiness, love, prosperity, wealth, riches, abundance, perfect health, success, and favor <u>over</u> your child <u>and to</u> your child daily, as soon as you learn that your child is on the way!

What You Say To Your Child as he or she (not "it") is physically developing inside the womb, after birth, and even until death do you part, will remain with your child and his or her children, and their children, and their children's children, henceforth and forever more.

This book is all about breaking family curses and generational curses that may have plagued your family for countless generations. It is my prayer that you will, after reading this book, come to realize that you might be the first person in your family to establish Generational Blessings that will continue until the end of this world, and beyond—even into Eternity!!!

The Guiding Scriptures That Are The Guiding Theme Of The Book

1. As for me, this is my covenant with them, saith the Lord; my spirit that is upon thee, and my words which I have put in thy mouth, shall not depart out of thy mouth, nor out of the mouth of thy seed, nor out of the mouth of thy seed's seed, saith the Lord, from henceforth and forever (Isaiah 59:21).

2. And these words, which I command thee this day, shall

be in thine heart; and thou shalt teach them diligently unto thy children and shalt talk of them when thou sittest in thine house, and when thou walkest by the way, and when thou liest down, and when thou risest up, and thou shalt bind them for a sign upon thine hand, and they shall be as frontlets between thine eyes. And thou shalt write them upon the posts of thy house, and on thy gates (Deuteronomy 6:6-9).

3. But speak thou the things which become sound doctrine: that the aged men be sober, grave, temperate, sound in faith, in charity, in patience. The aged women likewise, that they be in behavior as becoming holiness, not false accusers, not given to much wine, teachers of good things, that they may teach the young women to be sober, to love their husbands, to love their

children, to be discreet, chaste, keepers at home, good, obedient to their own husbands, that the word of God be not blasphemed. Young men likewise exhort to be sober minded in all things, shewing thyself a pattern of good works, in doctrine, shewing uncorruptness, gravity, sincerity, sound speech that cannot be condemned, that he that is of the contrary part may be ashamed, having no evil thing to say of you (Titus 2:1-8).

4. But this book of the law shall not depart out of thy mouth, but thou shalt meditate therein day and night, that thou mayest observe to do according to all that is written therein. For then thou shalt make thy way prosperous, and then thou shalt have good success (Joshua 1:8).

5. But what saith it? The word is nigh thee, even in thy mouth, and

in thy heart, that is, the word of faith, which we preach. That if thou shalt confess with thy mouth the Lord Jesus, and shalt believe in thine heart that God hath raised Him from the dead, thou shalt be saved. For with the heart man believeth unto righteousness, and with the mouth confession is made unto salvation. For the Scripture saith, whosoever believeth on Him shall not be ashamed (Romans 10:8-13).

Part One

The Power of Words

Words have power to either empower one to reach his or her maximum potential or to render one so helpless, hopeless, and incapacitated, he or she will never flourish, blossom, or thrive, even under the most positive of conditions or circumstances.

The Bible says that ""death and life are in the power of the tongue and that those who love it shall eat the fruit thereof" (Proverbs 18:21). You are at this very moment a sum total of words that have been heaped upon you for as long as you have existed in your mother's womb up to this present moment of time!

Imagine walking in your house one day, from the living room to the dining room, when it suddenly and abruptly dawns on you how successful, prosperous, rich, and wealthy you could be right now, today, if everyone you knew had lovingly, caringly, nurturingly, and dotingly spoken words of blessings, love, healing, success, happiness, and joy <u>over</u> you and <u>to</u> you for the past fifty years of your life, as they had and still do over others they know?

Imagine what it would feel like to be a lone ranger as you struggled every day of your fifty years on earth trying to "go it alone" and bless yourself because no one else who would have, should have and could have, did not.

If you have ever been in such a predicament, you probably began to wonder why everyone you knew blatantly and unashamedly went out of their way to speak well of everyone except you.

Then it also dawns on you why everyone was being blessed but you. You, believe it or not, are more blessed than everyone else that is being blessed by everyone else combined!!!!!!! This all important discovery, you will discover as I did, was only a set up for you to discover the power of just one blessing!!!!

One blessing contains within itself more power to bless you than a zillion curses combined, which was sent out like a posse to curse you.

For example, if you walk out to your mailbox one day to see a flurry of pennies in front of it, it does not take a genius to figure out that someone you know had sent a money curse to your house.

In such a case, it might be easy to get upset and bent out of shape about the money curse itself, until you realize one important truth: If someone sent a money curse to your house, it means you were never meant to experience a money blessing. No one can curse your money unless you actually possessed a money blessing.

On the same token, each word you speak to your baby, now and forever, is either setting up your child to walk under a blessing in a blessed state where blessings are the norm, or each word is setting up your child to walk under a curse in a cursed state, where curses seem to be a way of life.

All too often, parents, caregivers, and family members have no clue how harmful their negative words are when spoken. If just one negative word or comment is spoken repeatedly, recurrently, frequently, and habitually until it becomes a part of your child's mental psyche, it might take your child years just to undo the negative impact and emotional damage of such adverse words.

Telling your child that he or she is "stupid," "crazy", "bad" or "the devil" is detrimental to your child's overall academic, emotional, financial, mental, physical, sexual, social, and spiritual health.

What is even worse is that while you were speaking such words of negativity <u>over</u> and <u>to</u> your child, it would have been easier to say, "You are gifted!" You are a genius! "You are so good!" And you are an angel!"

In the latter case, had you called your child an angel, etcetera, he or she might have grown up to become the world's first Multi-Trillionaire to be featured in Forbes Magazine.

Moreover, had you said to your child, "You have a great future ahead of you," instead of saying, "You will never amount to anything," maybe your child would not have to settle for working on a minimum wage job earning $7.45 an hour, while others are making millions of dollars an hour in a legitimate, authentic, and genuine business.

What You Say to Your Child Really Does Matter was written for several vital reasons:

- To assist each first-time parent to learn and teach his or her child the value of establishing a healthy, life-long pattern of speaking words of perpetual blessings that can be successfully emulated and imitated for eternity, for successive generations.

- To assist individuals who feel shortchanged from a lack of edification and verbal praise, adulation, and acclamation to go back into time (the Spirit is timeless), to read, hear, verbalize and articulate all the spoken words they could have heard, should have heard, and would have heard in order to catch up and make up for lost time.

- To assist parents who want a better and higher standard of living for their child than what they themselves experienced, in giving their children a successful head start in life by teaching them to decree, declare, and visualize the life they want to have in advance while still in the womb. Note: It would be highly interesting to see how much more advanced your child would be post birth if he or she had been deliberately programmed with such words of blessings for nine months versus those children in the womb who had not.

- To assist anyone in life who has a sincere desire to become a serious blesser, with the goal and objective of making daily blessing God, themselves, others, persons, and things a life-long lifestyle that will attract more and more people, places, and things to bless perpetually, thus breaking a myriad of family, generational, and word curses that were on course to destroy the human race.

*******Note: Speaking well of everyone, everything, and every place, every day, around the clock, is a powerful way of breaking curses sent against you!!!

What better way to give your child a head start in life than by speaking well of your child even while he or she is still in the womb during embryonic, fetal, prenatal development, and post-natal development throughout the toddler stage, the childhood stage, the adolescent stage, and the adulthood stage.

Some experts have labeled such stages of postnatal development in various manners. One of those ways, according to Anatomy Answers, suggests that "the five life stages of postnatal development are: 1) neonatal, 2) infancy, 3) childhood, 4) adolescence, and 5) maturity.

The neonatal period extends from birth to one month. Infancy begins at one month and continues to two years of age. Childhood begins at two years of age and lasts until adolescence. Adolescence begins at around 12 or 13 years of age and ends with the beginning of adulthood. Adulthood, or maturity, includes the years between ages 18 to 25 and old age. The process of aging is called senescence."

For all practical purposes, I am sure that each child developmental, prenatal, and other related specialists would have their own timeline as to what constitutes each stage of development.

The important thing to know is that regardless of when each stage of prenatal and postnatal stages begins, it is of the utmost importance to maintain a healthy, blessed, happy, charismatic, enriching, empowering, enabling, and on-going dialogue with, to, and for your child for an eternity, starting in the womb!!! *What You Say To Your Child Really Does Matter*!!!

It has taken me fifty years to realize I was more blessed than those who were cursing me, my money, my jobs, my career, my raises, my promotions, my health, my body, my car, my relationships, my thanksgiving, my praise, my worship, my education, my business, my college degrees, my engagement, my future marriage, and my future, not to mention my past and present.

As it turns out, in the Spirit Realm and in the physical realm, I was to have the more abundant money, relationships, etcetera, according to 1 Corinthians 12.

It is my goal that you will find out the real truth of how blessed you are at this very moment, so you will not have to spend the next fifty years of your life spinning your wheels trying to break free of every curse under the sun.

What is not blessed is cursed, and it is also my objective that your child will not have to spend the rest of his or her life on earth, living in a cursed state, because no one cared enough to speak blessings to him or her daily.

As parents, *What You Say To Your Child Really Does Matter!!!* If you do not believe just how powerful your every word really is, just go down to the local Primary School and volunteer to work in the Kindergarten class during recess.

If a daughter's mother is the "bossy one" in the family, dominating her apparently weak, hen-pecked husband, the young girl in question will be observed bossing all the boys in the class around.

If a young, impressionable boy sees his mother getting slapped around by his dad, during recess that boy might say something to this effect: "If you do not do what I say, you know what is going to happen!!!!!"

Thank God, what has been learned can be unlearned. That is the first concept I learned in my Educational Psychology class when I was majoring in Education, beginning in 1991.

But, for all practicality, the purpose of *What You Say To Your Child Really Does Matter*, and I cannot emphasize that title and concept enough, is to empower you to sow the right kind of words that will usher your child into greatness!!!!

The affirmations that will come later in Part Two of this book are words that you should say to your child, beginning in the womb. Your baby, even though he or she is still in the prenatal stage of development, possesses a Spirit that is fully intact, and is fully operational at this point.

We all are Spirit Beings, living in a physical body, and we have a living soul that is able to think, reason, dream, create, and comprehend.

True, the Spirit within your child can be further nourished and developed throughout his or her life at will, yet, when it comes to your child, his or her Spirit completely sees, hears, and understands everything taking place within his or her, and your immediate living space.

Every word you speak to your baby, both inside the womb, now, and outside the womb after birth, is absorbed by your child like a sponge and is taken to heart.

As a result, by the time your baby is born, his or her personality, disposition, temperament, nature, make-up, persona, and outlook on life is pretty much already locked in, defined, and is obviously in place.

If you speak words of fear throughout your pregnancy, your child may be born with a fearful spirit that causes him or her to have either a noticeable, completely rigid and stiff body posture, or a fearful personality and/or fearful thought patterns and conversations and dialogues.

If you speak words of love and happiness, your child may appear to be friendly, even to strangers, because he or she subconsciously believes and assumes the whole universe is as full of love and happiness as well.

If you are always nervous about not having money to take care of your most basic of needs, your child may be born with a fear of lack that can never be broken.

If you are always speaking negatively about money, your child will incorporate such harmful and destructive words into his or her own subconscious mind.

If you have a lack of money, for whatever reason, instead of addressing the obvious shortage or deficiency of funds, say something along these lines: "We have plenty of money to pay the bills, with plenty of money left over to enjoy, save, spend, and invest!!!" "No matter how much it costs, we can afford it!!!" We are a high income family!!!"

Instead of complaining about a recession, depression, or a bad economy, you could say the following: "I bless the economy!!!" "We live in God's Infinite Economy where there is an overflow of riches, wealth, money, and abundance around the clock!!!"

Adding the enriching Scripture from Ephesians 3:20 would help tremendously: "God is able to do exceeding abundantly above all that we can ask or think."

Imagine what it would be like if your child growing inside the womb was born with an unseen, invisible, supernatural and Spiritual belief system that he or she is destined for greatness, and was born to be happy, successful, blessed, rich, prosperous, abundant, wealthy, perfectly healthy, wise, full of the Holy Ghost, and full of the Holy Spirit???

What if your child was born with the belief system that he or she was born to reign with Christ on the earth as Princes and Kings (Males) and as Princesses and Queens (Females)?

Your child knowing that he or she was born into a Spiritually Royal Family, and that he or she was born to reign with Christ is dependent upon you teaching him or her that truth while he or she is still inside the womb!!!

Certainly such knowledge of his or her Royalship would change the way your child walks in the earth, upon the earth, and how he or she goes about his Royal Business (The Father's Business),the Father being Jehovah Himself!!!

What your child believes about himself or herself and every-thing in his or her immediate surroundings will affect how he or she will live throughout his or her lifetime. For example, what career path will your child choose? (Being the "head and not the tail", meaning he or she will find opportunities to run businesses of his or her own, or land a job as president, Chief Executive Officer (CEO), or Chief Financial Officer (CFO) of the company, making so much more money than minimum wage).

In fact, the difference between your child working 25 hours a week at $7.43 an hour on a low-paying job versus earning $400,000 a year as does the current President of the United States of America, is all in *What You Say To Your Child Really Does Matter!!!*

Whatever you call such a phenomenon or occurrence—Early Childhood Development, Human Growth and Development, Child Development, Prenatal Development, Postnatal Development, Neonatal Development, General Psychology, Child Psychology, Developmental Psychology, Mind Science, Cognitive Behavior, Biblical Programming, Biblical Studies, Biblical Meditation, Spiritual Resources Management, Christian Education, Head Start, or just plain ole Common Sense, you owe it to your child to lay a firm, solid foundation, NOW, while he or she is still inside the womb, preparing for his or her trip down the birth canal to begin his or her new, life-long journey into the place we call home!!!

For that reason, it is highly important that you be upbeat, relaxed, calm, peaceful, happy, and joyful about life during and throughout the nine months of your pregnancy—throughout each trimester.

It is natural for well-meaning parents to want better for their child than what they themselves had. For example, if you never went to college, you would or should want and expect your child to enroll in college and get a degree.

From the moment your child has been conceived in the womb, you should be planting the "When you grow up, you will go to college" speech and message seed into your child's Spirit.

Why? So often, parents and loved ones who never attended college will either resent their child when he or she does actually go to college, or they will make their child feel badly because he went to college.

Even worse, parents who did not attend college might never encourage their child to go to college at all, thus allowing and permitting their child to spiral down a path of a lifetime of regrets about how he or she could have had a better, richer, easier life. *What You Say To Your Child About Money And Education Really Does Matter!!!*

Furthermore, if you could never earn more than $10,000 on your job at any time in your life, you would or should expect for your child to at least try to land a job earning in access of $100,000 a year, without his or her having to resort to illegal activities to do so.

If you encourage your child to speak correctly about his or her financial psychology about money, he or she will not buy into the world's belief system that the only way to make money in the present economy is to sell drugs or themselves. Trust me, not everyone resorts to such tactics of making money illegally just to "get by." I am one of them!!!

I must interject here that the two immediate, preceding statements are coming from someone who knows what it is like to earn only $7.43 an hour as a home health assistant. The glory in such a financial history is that in all that time, not one time did I resort to selling drugs or booty to obtain money.

Consequently, you would not believe the incessant, unrelenting, ruthless and shrewd conversations I had to endure for years from family members, church members, clergy, acquaintances, and even strangers who insisted that thinking about and talking about money correctly, or thinking about having lots of money versus staying broke is a taboo.

Such hurtful, damaging, and dangerously, heart wrenching discussions are an abomination in the eyes of God, who is Infinitely rich and wealthy.

It should be preached on the roof of every housetop that it is an abomination, outrage, disgrace, horror, and an atrocity for everyone to tell anyone that "It is not God's Will for you to have money."

For anyone to make such an ungodly remark is a shrewd attempt to keep a person in a permanent cycle of poverty, lack, and insufficiency, which goes against the grain of God's rich and abundant creation called earth.

Telling your child that "It is God's Will for him or her to have plenty of money" is in fact Biblical. Even Jesus told Peter to go fishing and that he would find money to pay both their taxes in the mouth of the first fish he caught. Does that sound like God wants you to be living from paycheck to paycheck, barely having enough money to pay attention?

That is why it is indeed important that you say the right things to your child about money. If you and everyone in your child's life believe that it is a sin or a social taboo to have money, to be rich, or to be wealthy, your child is getting the wrong script to follow for life.

Moreover, if your child has to swim upstream as I did and have to spend over ten years learning how to program your subconscious mind to receive Infinite Wealth and Infinite Money no one you know wants you to have, then, no one should go out of his or her way trying to find out how you managed to attract all the money and wealth you were never supposed to have when you actually get it!!!

If you have not already figured it out, I am a published author and novelist, and you would be surprised how difficult it was to publish any of my preceding books, due to everyone's unwillingness for me to complete any of these publications.

I was under a lot of stress typing any of my manuscripts after 1:00 p.m. After working only 25 hours a week, Monday through Friday, my going to the library to complete my books, (all of which deal with having astronomical self-confidence and wealth), was my full-time attempt to earn more than $10,000 a year.

Subsequently, many of my manuscripts were movie deal potential, and I had two opportunities to travel to Los Angeles and to Las Vegas to speak to movie producers about turning my books into a movie.

Unfortunately, such doors were closed due to other people's unwillingness to help me become financially successful. Yet, on the other hand, everyone I knew went out of their way to tell me 50 Million reasons why I would not land movie deals.

So as you can see, it has been a struggle to encourage myself to become my own nurturing parent. At this particular moment, I am indeed proud to share with you a host of synonyms and a few antonyms of the word, "nurturing, that I found on Thesaurus.com. These words are not listed in any alphabetical order and many of the words are repeated more than once for extra emphasis:

"Cultural, educational, enlightening, adorning, advancing, artistic, beautifying, beneficial, broadening, civilizing, constructive, corrective, developmental, dignifying, disciplining, edifying, educative, elevating, enabling, enriching, expanding, glorifying, helpful, humane, humanizing, influential, inspirational, instructional, learned, liberalizing, nurturing, ornamenting, polishing, promoting, raising, refined, refining, regenerative, socializing, stimulating, uplifting, widening, motherly, bring up, raise youngster, breed, cultivate, develop, educate, feed, form, foster, nourish, provide for, rear, school, support, teach, train, care for, tend to, attend, babysit, consider, keep an eye on, keep tabs on, look after, mind, mind the store, minister, mother, nurse, pay attention to, protect, sit, take pains, tend, treasure, wait on, watch, watch over, motherly, caring, affectionate, careful, caretaking, comforting, devoted, fond, gentle, kind, loving, maternal, nurturing, protecting, protective, sheltering, supporting, sympathetic, tender, warm, watchful, cherish, care about deeply, admire, adore, appreciate, apprize, care for, clasp, cleave to, cling to, coddle, comfort, cosset, defend, dote on, embrace, encourage, enshrine, entertain, fancy, foster, guard, harbor, hold dear, hold in high esteem, honor, hug, idolize, love, nurse, pet, preserve, prize, revere, reverence, safeguard, shelter, shield, support, sustain, treasure, value, venerate, and worship.

Cherish means to be fond of, be attached to, while **nurture** means to bring up, help develop, help grow, or provide with nourishment."

The Power Of "Nurturing" Words!!!

Notice the antonyms of the word, nourishing: "to denounce, renounce, abandon, forsake, and not care." That is what parents, caregivers, or anyone responsible for your child's education do when they fail to nurture a child.

That is what you will do <u>to</u> your child if you fail to speak blessings <u>to</u> your child on a daily basis, before and after life inside the womb!!!

That is what will happen if you fail to speak well <u>of</u> your child and fail to give him or her the invaluable resource of learning to bless himself or herself consistently.

If on the other end of the spectrum, in getting back to *What You Say To Your Child Really Does Matter*, concerning money, riches, wealth and success, if you had run a successful business for years, you should expect your child to own multiple franchises or an innumerable, myriad of chain stores.

Likewise, if you earned a whopping $1 Million a day, you should expect your child to earn at least $1 Billion a day, if not $1 Trillion.

The Word says, "A good man [woman] leaveth an inheritance to his children's children." Consequently, if you die today and leave your child broke and penniless, thinking he or she should "find their own way," you have fallen short of God's Word and God's Glory!!!!

In such a case, you could not blame your falling short of what God said on bad luck, a bad economy, a bad marriage, bad parenting skills, a lack of knowledge, misunderstanding or miscommunication.

If God said we all are to leave an inheritance for our children's children, He could and would bypass our present American and Global Economy to get His child all that wealth.

Part of that system is contained within *What You Say To Your Child Really Does Matter!!!* It has been said that "there is no day like the present!!!

Today, not tomorrow, not next week, not next month, not next year, and certainly not five, ten, fifty, or a hundred years from now, is the day you can begin to deliberately say to your child that he or she is blessed, successful, rich, wealthy, abundant, prosperous, happy, loved, wanted, cherished, and adored!!!

As parents, adoptive parents, and/or caregivers, it is your sole responsibility to nurture, emotionally support, provide for, take care of, discipline (correctly), correct (appropriately), and show love

31

and adoration to your child around the clock.

Above all things, it is important that you bless your child daily and say great things about him or her that will build in him or her self-love, self-respect, self-confidence, self-esteem, self-worth, and self-dignity, not to mention self-appreciation.

In the church world, members are taught to be humble, meek, and kind, and not to think more highly of themselves than they ought to think. Might I remind you that there is a great difference between being humble and exhibiting self-confidence.

No one, especially you, should be teaching your child how to be somebody's victim, somebody's doormat, somebody's flunky, and somebody's punching bag!!!!

Should you follow the affirmations contained within this book, starting today, you are giving your children the ability to attract healthy relationships with the opposite sex, and to attract his and her soul mates who will add to his or her life rather than diminishing it.

The bottom line??? The answer could not be any more easier or clearer!!! *What You Say to Your Child Really Will Matter* when it comes down to whom your child will marry, and whether or not he or she is financially compatible with his or her soul mate.

No one should marry a dead-beat man who will not lift a finger to support his family financially. Your child and his or her own child should not have to fend for themselves monetarily or financially!!!

Teach your child to marry well off to a spouse who is well off financially. Treat your child with respect and dignity, so they will be treated well before, during, and throughout the marriage.

Teach your child one important fact: What he or she says to himself or herself, and about himself or herself consistently on a daily basis really will affect them, <u>and</u> his or her child as well as his or her children and their children's children.

If you fail to bless your child, while you child is in the womb, NOW, it may take them the next fifty years of his or her natural life, wondering around in life aimlessly under so many family, generational, word, money, house, marriage, and career curses, he or she might never break free.

In short, teach your child to bless God, themselves, others, things, and teach them to curse the curses not so well-meaning cursers may send in his or her direction to undermine, shortchange, and hinder their God-Given, God-Ordained, God-Inspired, and God-Breathed Blessings!!!

Lastly, this book, *What You Say To Your Child Really Does Matter,* is not about you "finding Jesus" if you have not done so already, or you supposedly "getting saved", or you converting to a particular religion.

Whether you are a Catholic, Christian, Jew, Atheist, Hindu, Buddhist, Muslim, Mormon, Jehovah's Witness, or Seventh Day Adventist, *What You Say To Your Child*, starting upon the very second of conception until death do you part, *Really Does Matter!!!*

What You Say To Your Child about money *Really Does Matter!!!* Always speak positively about money in the presence of your child, and even behind his or her back, backing up your every word with correct action.

Every word you speak to your child about money will go with him or her for the rest of his or her natural life. Long after you have gone, what you have said to him or her about money today, and every day will leave a lasting, and virtually unbreakable, permanent impression.

What You Say To Your Child about his or her royal status in life *Really Does Matter!!!* Teach your child to daily think of himself or herself as a royal Prince, King, Princess, or Queen, and you will definitely ensure that your child will attract healthy relationships with the opposite sex that may ultimately lead to "they got married and lived happily ever after!!!"

When your child learns to think highly of himself or herself in the most powerful, positive way, he or she will attract his or her soul mate versus "just a mate, who will treat him or her just any kind of way."

What You Say To Your Child about education *Really Does Matter!!!* Life is just that—a life-long process. One never reaches the point where he or she "has arrived." There is always more to learn. Sometimes, you may even have to re-think what you think you already know just to learn a new concept.

Additionally, George Beverly Shaw made this statement that was often quoted by both President John F. Kennedy and Robert Kennedy during their campaigns: "Some people see things as they are and ask, 'Why not?' I dream things that never were and ask, 'Why Not?'"

In my mind, this is the ultimate utopian, self-actualized statement that anyone can ascribe to!!! A real education begins when your child realizes that he or she was born to *think outside the box, and not to mention color outside the lines of conventional, traditional, mundane, mediocre forms of thought.*

The Apostle Paul said these words in 1 Corinthians 2:9-10: "Eye hath not seen, nor ear heard, neither have entered into the heart of man, the things that God hath prepared for them that hove him. But they are revealed unto him by the spirit." When it comes to your child, God may have plans to do for him or her things that no one anywhere on the planet has even thought about, let alone accomplished!!!

What You Say To Your Child about living accommodations Really Does Matter!!! Everything you say and do will affect where your child will live, how he or she will live, and in what kind of housing he or she will dwell.

Teach your child that having lots of money in life is wrong, and he or she will try to bargain himself or herself into less than royalty housing. If you had led your child to believe that he or she was less than royalty and that times are tough in our present-day economy, he or she might settle for subsidy housing instead, just to save the taxpayers money.

No King or Queen would even consider reigning from anywhere but a palace or castle. Queen Elizabeth primarily resides in Buckingham

Palace, though she has more luxurious estates.

The Presidents of the United States dwell in the White House at 1600 Pennsylvania Avenue. And in your child's case, would he or she live in a mansion? If so, how many mansions would he or she live in, and how much would each one cost?

The answer to that question lies in *What You Say To Your Child!!! What You Say To Your Child Really Does Matter!!! What you Say To Your Child* today will determine how successful your child will be today, tomorrow, and for the rest of his or her life!!!

No one ever comes into the presence of a king or queen without bowing upon coming directly in front of the throne, before leaving the presence of the king or queen, or even after the queen or king has made a royal decree.

If you want your child to be a great success, speak well of your child, to your child, <u>for</u> your child, <u>with</u> your child, <u>in front of</u> your child, <u>behind</u> your child, and <u>beside</u> your child, as if they are kings, princes, queen, and princesses living in a royal palace.

In closing, the affirmations contained within *What You Say To Your Child Really Does Matter*, is not the means to an end. These declarations are not the only scripts, self-talk, or Biblical Programming and Biblical Meditations that you have at your disposal.

These declarative statements are the scripts I used to get from Point A to Point B in the fastest amount of time in order to make up for lost time, and to gain valuable ground in catching up to where I could have been, should have been, and would have been if those loved ones in my life had followed the advice in this book.

As you are faithful in lovingly speaking these words to your child, you will be given higher forms of affirmations that are guaranteed to work for you and your child even faster.

Adopt these words as your lifestyle, and do not judge them because they appear to be Spiritual in nature. "God has blessed us with all Spiritual Blessings in heavenly places" (Ephesians 1:3), meaning everything your child needs and will ever need or want must first come from the Spirit where every good things dwell.

"Out of your belly shall flow rivers of living water" (John 7:38). God wants your child to "have life and have it more abundantly" according to John 10:10.

Speak life to your child!!! Speak love to your child!!! Speak happiness to your child!!! Speak "Life is easy" to your child so that your child will have it easy!!! It is imperative that you tell your child how easy life is so life will be easy for them, and not a chore, bother, or hassle. Life for them should be easier than what you experienced in your own life.

What You Say To Your Child today and every day for the rest of your life, until death do you part, *Really Does Matter!!!*

God bless you and your child, and may you and your child continue to bless God, yourselves, each other, others, and things henceforth and forever more.

Love,

Lisa Lee Hairston

Mother of Nations!!!

Part Two

The Power of
Affirmations!!!

What You Say To Your Child Really Does Matter!!! In Part One, you were given a head start in learning the power of the spoken word and why what you say to your child is of the most upmost importance. What you say to your child NOW, beginning in the womb, will dictate the success or failure of your child today, and the rest of his or her life, not to mention future generations.

In this section, I have deliberately given you the most powerful affirmations that I would use if I were to go back into my life to give myself a head start in life.

If you have not guessed by now, I already have gone back into time to bathe, soak in, and absorb all the words I would want to hear today if I were having a normal conversation with anyone, into my psyche. At the present moment, I am ecstatic in this new venture in my life.

My God, Jehovah, is a King, and he sits on his royal throne in heaven and in my heart as well. I now realize that my true calling in life is to be a blessing to everyone I meet.

To make a long story short, one day, about three weeks ago, God told me that I was a Princess and a Queen, and that I was "Born Again" Spiritually to reign with Christ on the earth.

When God asked me what I would want to do if He were reigning on the throne daily, seated next to Christ, and I was engaged in performing my royal duties as Princess or Queen, I imagined that I would spend one whole day blessing everyone who stood before me as I sat on the throne.

I had so much fun with this visualization exercise, I kept up the blessing technique, and the daily affirmations that follow are the result. Of course, I had no idea at the time that even thinking about reigning with Christ would change my life forever.

I feel as if I have experienced somewhat of a "New Birth" mentioned in John 3 when Jesus said to Nicodemus, "You must be Born Again." Additionally, in 2 Corinthians 5:17, we are told, "If any man be in Christ, he is a new creature. Old things have passed away, and behold the new are come!!!"

Wow, do I feel new!!! And so will you as you begin in this section to apply what you have learned in Part One. Please be advised that the words, affirmations, statements, declarations, assertions, pronouncements, confirmations, and verifications contained within the next few pages are only a Spiritual guide to get you and your baby started off on the right foot!!!

As you proceed in employing the affirmations I highly recommend, you will discover other positive affirmations of your own to assist you in your life-long journey of communicating richly and positively with your beloved child.

Lastly, you will also discover that there are so many venues and avenues of possible topics of interest—from how to handle money to how to find your soul mate.

Always remember that your child is an imitator and the words you speak to him or her on a daily basis, concerning any matter will, whether they are positive or negative, inspire your child to want to grow up and be just like you!!!

With that said, what will your child grow up to be as a result of the total sum of words you have deposited into his or her psyche and Spirit? *What You Say To Your Child Really Does Matter!!!*

Daily Welcome Affirmation For Your Baby!!!

Welcome into my life, little one!!! You are my pride and joy, and I have a few words of wisdom that I want you to always remember about life—words that you can only hear from us.

As your parents, it is our sole responsibility to nurture you, emotionally support you, listen to you, advise you, counsel you, correct you, guide you, and take care of you academically, emotionally, financially, mentally, physically, sexually (make sure you are comfortable with your sexual, heterosexual orientation), socially, and spiritually, until you are old enough to move out on your own, buy your first place, get married, and begin your own family.

Even after such a transitional moment, we will always be here for you, as long as we both shall live, to love you, encourage you, motivate you, inspire you, befriend you, help you, and stimulate your brain with new scintillating ideas!!!

What we are about to say to you are words of wisdom that perhaps no one else you know would want to share with you for various reasons. These words reflect the person you were born to be, the life you were destined to live, and the plans God has for your very existence.

The nature of these words also reflects how you should communicate with God, yourself, us, and others on a daily basis, irrespective of what others around you are saying and doing. *You* *are what you <u>say about</u> yourself daily!!! You are what you <u>think of</u> yourself daily!!! You are what you <u>believe about</u> yourself daily!!!*

Say the right things about yourself daily, think of yourself correctly daily, and believe the best about yourself daily, and you will always have the power and the capacity to rise up above all negativity the world may and will try to impose upon you.

These words we are about to impart unto you are words directly from the heart of God to yours. These are the words the people who know you best would never adopt as their own philosophy!!!

Meditate on these words daily, follow the wisdom of these words daily, and you will find yourself "living far above all principality <u>and</u> power, <u>and</u> might, <u>and</u> dominion, <u>and</u> every name that is named, not only in this world but in that which is to come" (Ephesians 1:21)—a world (Infinite Economy) which exceeds our present day economy!!!

Lastly, we speak these words directly to your Spirit, our little one, as you develop and grow inside the womb. In doing so, we are ensuring that you have a Spiritual head start in life before you are born into this earth realm we call home. By the time of your arrival, you will be able to function the way God intended, and not the way the world will insist that you live!!!

Life Is Easy!!!

The world will try to convince you that life is hard. According to Proverbs 13:15, "The way of transgressors is hard." To translate, life should only be hard for those who transgress God's Law and God's Word.

The following affirmations are designed to be spoken <u>to</u> you and <u>over</u> you, NOW, while you are in the womb, so that you will always remember that life is easy!!! In the words of Jesus, "Be it done to you according to your faith." The more you meditate, NOW, on how easy life is, the easier life will be by the time you are born into the earth realm.

Our saying the words, "Life Is Easy," to you today, at this special moment in your life *really does matter.* It will affect how you conduct yourself throughout your life. If you believe that life is easy, you will have an easy life, and you can and will live on easy street, regardless of what is happening around you.

Lastly, along these lines, the Bible tells you in Romans 12:2, "And be not conformed to this world, but be ye transformed by the renewing of your mind, that you may prove what is that good, acceptable, and perfect will of God."

You are what the Word says you are!!! You can <u>be</u> what the Word says you can be!!! You can <u>do</u> what the Word says you can do!!! And you can <u>have</u> what the Word says you can have!!!

If the Word says you can have it easy . . . If the Word says you can live on Easy Street . . . You absolutely can!!! The world will never accept that as your reality. So take God at His Word, and believe that you were born to have it easy in life. Enjoy the following Affirmations and make sure you say them, ponder on them, and meditate on them daily:

Life Is Easy Affirmations!!!

Life Is Easy!!!

Finding The Right Career Is Easy!

Starting A Successful
Business Is Easy!

Finding Your True Calling
In Life Is Easy!

Obtaining And Receiving Your
Perfect Salary Is Easy!

Making A Lot Of Money Is Easy!

Making Your First Million Is Easy!

Making Your First Billion Is Easy!

Making Your First Trillion Is Easy!

Becoming A Multi-Trillionaire Is Easy!

Becoming A Millionaire Is Easy!

Becoming A Billionaire Is Easy!

Becoming A Trillionaire Is Easy!

Thinking Like A Centillionaire Is Easy!

Having the Right Financial
Psychology About Money Is Easy!

Paying All Your Bills Each Month With
Plenty Of Money Left Over Is Easy!

Having A Lot Of Money Is Easy!

Living At Your Privilege Is Easy!

Getting Substantial Raises Is Easy!

Getting Hefty Money Bonuses Is Easy!

Getting Prominent Promotions
On The Job Is Easy!

Living On Easy Street, Where
Everything Is Easy, Is Easy!

Buying Your First Mansion Is Easy!

Buying Your First Sports Car Is Easy!

Buying Your First Luxury Car Is Easy!

Acquiring Large Estates Is Easy!

Going Into Real Estate Is Easy!

Walking In The Spirit Is Easy!

Living In The Spirit Is Easy!

Living In Christ Is Easy!

Living For Christ Is Easy!

Living With Christ Is Easy!

Thanking God Is Easy!

Praising God Is Easy!

Worshipping God Is Easy!

Ministering Directly To God Is Easy!

Believing God Is Easy!

Receiving From God Is Easy!

Marrying Your Soul Mate Is Easy!

Marrying the Love Of Your Life Is Easy!

Having The Wedding Day
You Dream Of Is Easy!

Having A Marriage Made
In Heaven Is Easy!

Having A Happy Marriage Is Easy!

Achieving Great Emotional Intimacy
With Your Spouse Is Easy!

Having A Great Academic
Career Is Easy!

Getting Your First Doctorate Is Easy!

Having Friends In High Places Is Easy!

Life Is Good!!!

My child, there are many people in the world with what can only be described as "the bad luck syndrome." These are the folk who are so obsessed with, and full of the thought of bad things happening to them daily, they only attract what they perceive as bad luck.

What these good people do not know, and never seem to find out, is one simple, but obvious truth: choosing to think about all the good things that can and will occur daily will have the same powerful and positive "good luck syndrome" effect!!!

My child, good thoughts and bad thoughts, as well as good luck and bad luck, cannot and will not dwell in one place under one roof, or within you simultaneously. You can deliberately choose one syndrome over the other by deciding which of the two you will follow.

Today, and every day for the rest of your life, you can choose to affirm these words both silently and out loud, "Life is GOOD!!!"

If you will be faithful in speaking forth these three simple words, 24 hours a day, 7 days a week, and 365 days of the year, 366 days in leap year, you will not be able to stop all the good things that will happen to you daily!!!

Life Is Good Affirmations!!!

Go one step farther and declare the rest of these affirmations as well. "Call those things that be not as though they were (Romans 4:17):

Life Is Good!!!

I Feel Good!!!

I Look Good!!!

I Smell Good!!!

I Am Living Good In The Neighborhood!!!

I Am Being Treated Good In The Neighborhood!!!

I Have Good Money!!!

I Have A Good Job!!!

I Have A Good Career!!!

I Have A Good Business!!!

I Have A Good Husband!!!

I Have A Good Wife!!!

I Have A Good Child!!!

I Have Good Children!!!

I Married A Good Man!!!

I Married A Good Woman!!!

I Have A Good Home!!!

I Have A "Goodly" House!!!

I Have Good Credit!!!

I Have Good Friends!!!

I Have A Good Education!!!

I Have Good Credentials!!!

I Have A Good Name!!!

I Have A Good Reputation!!!

I Have Good Character!!!

I Have Good Character References!!!

I Have A Good Resume!!!

I Live In A Good Neighborhood!!!

I Had A Good Childhood!!!

I Am A Good Woman!!!

I Am A Good Man!!!

I Am A Good Girl!!!

I Am A Good Boy!!!

I Am Doing Good!!!

My Husband Is Doing Good!!!

My Wife Is Doing Good!!!

My Child Is Doing Good!!!

My Family Is Doing Good!!!

I Am Having It Good!!!

Good Things Are Always
Happening To Me!!!

Something Good Is Going To
Happen To Me Today!!!

Something Good Is Going To
Happen To Me Tomorrow!!!

Something Good Is Going To
Happen To Me This Week!!!

Something Good Is Going To
Happen To Me This Month!!!

Something Good Is Going To
Happen To Me This Year!!!

Something Good Is Going To
Happen To Me At Work!!!

Something Good Is Going To
Happen To Me On The Job!!!

Something Good Is Going To
Happen To Me At Church!!!

No matter what I do, no matter
where I go, and no matter where
my feet shall tread, something good
always happens to me, because I
always expect for GOOD THINGS to
happen to me, and for me!!! Someone
is always putting in a good word for me
edge-wise!!!

Life Is Sweet!!!

As you have heard from us, my child, life is easy, life is good, and now you are about to learn that life is sweet!!! Consider these words coming from Psalms 34:8, "O taste and see that the Lord is Good!!!"

If you were to listen diligently to the Iron Chefs on the Food Network Show, you would know that they are absolutely geniuses when it comes to extracting flavor in every hearty dish they prepare. They take great pleasure in bringing out sweet, sour, salty, and even bitter flavors that are palatable to the human taste and imagination.

Once you are born, you will discover that a few individuals have lost their ability to enjoy life. They have lost their zing and passion for what used to bring them joy. Life for them has become bitter-sweet, if not permanently sour.

When life handed them lemonades, they refused to add in the sweetness we call sugar to make refreshing lemonade. As your parents, we want to help you get started in life on the right foot!!! Always affirm these words, regardless of what the current situation is: "Life is sweet!!!" These words will take you far!!!

My child, life is not only good, life is not only easy, life is sweet!!! Those who say otherwise have for some reason allowed all the joy and sweetness to exit their life, as they choose to focus only on the bitter.

Let the words, "Life is sweet," be your daily confession. A life of sweetness is in the eye of the beholder.

Life Is Sweet
Affirmations!!!

Life Is Sweet!!!

Life Is Sweet Because The God That Reigns In Me Is Sweet On Me!!!

With Each Passing Second Of The Day, My Life Only Gets Sweeter!!!

The Universe Is Full Of Infinite Abundance!!!

No matter where you go anywhere on the earth—be it the east coast, the west coast, the farthest north, the deepest south, the seven continents, or beyond, the universe if full of Infinite Abundance.

How do we know? All the Abundance that can be seen belongs exclusively to God—The Infinite One who is very definite about how Infinitely Abundant you actually are!!!

According to the Scriptures, "The earth is the Lord's and the fullness thereof, the world, and all they that dwell therein" (Psalms 24:1). Those same Scriptures also say that "the cattle upon a thousand hills belong to God" (Psalms 50:10).

The whole earth, beginning at the moment of its conception and creation, was designed to display and reflect that Abundance. Everything else and anything else, seen or unseen, visible, or invisible, is only an illusion.

Also according to Scripture, "God is no respecter of persons(Acts 10:34), meaning that Abundance is available to everyone regardless of one's race, sex, gender, socio-economic status, or religious background.

Subsequently, there is no limitation as to how much Abundance you can have. As far as God is concerned, the Abundance that exists in Heaven (the riches of His Glory—Philippians 4:19) and the abundance in the earth, on the earth, is as Infinite as God!!!

My child, I pray that God would open both your physical eyes and your spiritual eyes to see all the Abundance within you, around you, and for you!!! The more you focus on such Infinite Abundance, and the more you focus on how Abundant The Infinite really is, the more Abundance you will have!!!

The Universe Is Full Of Infinite Abundance Affirmations!!!

I Am Surrounded By
Infinite Abundance!!!

I Am Full Of Infinite Abundance!!!

I Receive Infinite Abundance Daily!!!

I Have Plenty Of Infinite Abundance!!!

My Infinite Abundance
Is Running Over!!!

I Love Infinite Abundance!!!

And Infinite Abundance Loves Me!!!

I Give Thanks For The Infinite Abundance Within Me Now!!!

I Give Thanks That Jehovah God, The Infinite, Is My Source Of Infinite Abundance!!!

Only Sex Between A Husband And Wife Is Holy!!!

My child, you will do wise to heed the advice given directly by God Himself concerning the topic of sex: "Marriage is honourable in all, and the bed undefiled; but whoremongers and adulterers God will judge" (Hebrews 13:4).

The Amplified Bible says it thusly, "Let marriage be held in honor (esteemed worthy, precious, of great price, and especially dear) in all things. And thus let the marriage bed be undefiled (kept undishonored); for God will judge and punish the unchaste [all guilty of sexual vice] and adulterous."

Marriage is one of the greatest institutions God ever created! The Functional Family is everything to God. Within that Functional Family—within that Holy Sacred Marriage—God has sanctified sex between the husband and wife, set it apart, and glorified it so that sexual intimacy between spouses would bring Him exclusive Glory.

Unfortunately, many individuals—both men and women, both males and females, have transgressed this law. Many men find it foolish to be faithful to their wives, and many single women have been duped into this line of thinking from the man who refuses to honor the marriage vows: "I have to know what I am getting!!!"

Nothing could be further from the truth. As you rest in the womb, waiting for your entry into the earth realm, this is the perfect time for you to become acquainted with God's laws concerning the family, marriage, and sex between a husband and wife only.

If you step into the church world, you will hear pastors preaching relentlessly about such matters as fornication (sex between a single man and single woman), which is a great thing to preach about only if that kind of sermon is directed at the man who refuses to wait for marriage to want sex.

That kind of sermon is not so great if those committing adultery (those whom are married) are flying under the radar undetected. Subsequently, that same sermon is not so great, if everyone under the sound of the preacher's voice during the sermon leaves the church Sunday after Sunday believing that sex is something evil, nasty, dirty, or depraved.

Such depravity in discussing sex in the church in the manner described can only leave a bad taste in one's mouth, especially if the pastor has left the impression that sex even between a husband and wife is something to turn your nose up at.

My child, at all costs, keep yourself undefiled, pure, and holy, meaning wait until the wedding night to enjoy the gift of sex that God has lovingly given you as husband and wife. Anyone who does not want to wait until the wedding night for that Blessed Event is either selfish, self-centered, or does not really love you!!!

The following affirmations have been carefully chosen for you to affirm daily, beginning today, while you are still in the womb, so that you will have a healthy sex life, a healthy sexual orientation (heterosexual only), and a healthy view of sex that only sees sex from God's point of view. Anything else is merely an illusion!!!

Only Sex Between A Husband And Wife Is Holy Affirmations!!!

Sex Between A Husband And Wife Is Holy!!!

Sex Between A Husband And Wife Is Pure!!!

Sex Between A Husband And Wife Is Undefiled!!!

Sex Between A Husband And Wife Is Sacred!!!

Sex Between A Husband And Wife Is Unblemished!!!

Sex Between A Husband And
Wife Is Uninhibited!!!

Sex Between A Husband And
Wife Is Unadulterated!!!

Sex Between A Husband And
Wife Is Uncontaminated!!!

Sex Between A Husband
And Wife Is Untainted!!!

Sex Between A Husband
And Wife Is Anointed!!!

Sex Between A Husband And
Wife Is God-Ordained!!!

Sex Between A Husband And
Wife Is God-Approved!!!

Sex Between A Husband And
Wife Is God's Appointment!!!

Sex Between A Husband And
Wife Is Glorifying To God!!!

Sex Between A Husband And
Wife Is Sanctioned By God!!!

Sex Between A Husband And Wife Is God's Gift!!!

Sex Between A Husband And Wife Is A Gift Of God From God!!!

Sex Between A Husband And Wife Is Spiritual!!!

Sex Between A Husband And Wife Is Without Spot Or Wrinkle!!!

Sex Between A Husband And Wife Is Covered By The Blood Of The Lamb!!!

You Are A Blesser!!!

You are the most blessed forever (Psalms 13:15)!!! You are blessed in your going out, and you are blessed in your coming in according to Deuteronomy 28. You are so full of blessings until there is nothing satan can do to curse you.

No matter what you do in life, or where your life takes you on your earthly journey, one blessing is stronger than a million, billion, trillion, or centillion curses!!!

It really does matter what you bless, whom you bless, when you bless, how you bless, where you bless, and why you bless. You are to bless the Lord at all times(Psalms 34:1)You are to bless everyone, everything, and everybody, including yourself, at all times, until you can literally and truly say that blessing is a lifestyle.

Much has been said about the lifestyles of the rich and the famous, but not enough has been said about the lifestyles of the blesser!!! You are not blessed until you become a blesser.

For example, many people in the church world, especially, will tell you they are blessed when you ask them how they are doing, but that does not mean they want you blessed. In fact, those same people who say they are blessed may be secretly or openly cursing you, yet they will still maintain that they are blessed. Nothing can be further from the truth!!!

What such individuals mean when they tell you they are blessed is that God has been blessing them with physical and material blessings such as cars, houses, and land. They may have five cars in their yard, when they have no desire for you to even have one good car.

Dearly beloved, herein is the one secret to life: Become a blesser with a capital "B!!!" As the Bible says, "Go into your secret closet and bless God, yourself, others, and things "in secret so that God will bless you openly" (Matthew 6:6)

Then, and only then, will God consider you blessed. Make blessing your daily routine, practice, habit, and lifestyle. Listed below are just a few ways you can be a blessing to God, yourself, and others, as you go about your Heavenly Father's Blessing Business.

You Are A Blesser Affirmations!!!

Pray these prayers daily as if they are your book of prayers:

Bless You Mind!

Bless You Body!'

Bless You Upper Body!

Bless You Lower Body!

Bless You Soul!

Bless You Spirit!

Bless You Head!

Bless You Brains!

Bless You Hands!

Bless You Fingers!

Bless You Feet!

Bless You Toes!

Bless You Face!

Bless You Eyes!

Bless You Ears!

Bless You Hearing!

Bless You Mouth!

Bless You Lips!

Bless You Teeth!

Bless You Hair!

Bless You Tongue!

Bless You Breath!

Bless You Legs!

Bless You Hips!

Bless You Belly!

Bless You Back!

Bless You Heart!

Bless You Chest!

Bless You Breasts!

Bless You Knees

Bless You Shoulders!

Bless You Neck!

Bless You Skin!

Bless You Penis!

Bless You Prostrate!

Bless You Testicles!

Bless You Scrotum!

Bless You Vagina!

Bless You Clitoris!

Bless You Womb!

Bless You Ovaries

Bless You Uterus!

Bless You Vulva!

Bless You Female Genitals!

Bless You Male Genitals!

Bless You Sexual
Reproductive Organs!

Bless You Bones!

Bless You Muscles!

Bless You Tissues!

Bless You Healthy Cells!

Bless You Ligaments!

Bless You Tendons!

Bless You Organs!

Bless You Immune System!

Bless You Buttocks!

Bless You Money!

Bless You Wealth!

Bless You Riches!

Bless You Physical Blessings!

Bless You Spiritual Blessings!

Bless You Raises!

Bless You Promotions!

Bless You Perfect Salary!

Bless You Career!

Bless You Job!

Bless You Boss!

Bless You Supervisor!

Bless You Business!

Bless You House!

Bless You Mansion!

Bless You Estate!

Bless You Property!

Bless You Space!

Bless You Car!

Bless You Environment!

Bless You Atmosphere!

Bless You Surroundings!

Bless You Rich Universe!

Bless You Godly Wisdom!

Bless You Gifts Of The Spirit!

Bless You Fruits Of The Spirit!

Bless You God!

Bless You Jesus!

Bless You Holy Ghost!

Bless You Perfect Date!

Bless You Engagement!

Bless You Fiance (Females)

Bless You Fiancee (Males)

Bless You Help Meet!

Bless You Husband (Females)!

Bless You Wife (Males)!

Bless You Wedding Day!

Bless You Wedding Night!

Bless You Honeymoon!

Bless You Wedding Ceremony!

Bless You Wedding Rehearsal!

Bless You Wedding Reception!

Bless You Wedding Gifts!

Bless You Wedding Planner!

Bless You Wedding Vows!

Bless You Wedding Guests!

Bless You Wedding Invitations!

Bless You Wedding
Prenuptials(Optional)!

Bless You Wedding Gown!

Bless You Tuxedo!

Bless You Bride!

Bless You Maid Of Honor!

Bless You Bridesmaids!

Bless You Groom!

Bless You Best Men!

Bless You Ushers!

Bless You Caterers!

Bless You Wedding Attendants!

Bless You Homemaker!

Bless You Career Man!

Bless You Career Woman!

Bless You Entrepreneur!

Bless You Parents!

Bless You Children!

Bless You Life!

Bless You Happy Retirement!

Bless You Bank Accounts!

Bless You Checking Accounts!

Bless You Savings Accounts!

Bless You Money Market Accounts!

Bless You IRA's!

Bless You Certificates
Of Deposits (CD's)

Bless You Land!

Bless You Ground!

Bless You Property!

Bless You Femininity!

Bless You Womanhood!

Bless You Masculinity!

Bless You Manhood!

Bless You Sexuality!

Bless You Childbirth!

Bless You Childhood!

Bless You Adolescence!

Bless You Adulthood!

Bless You Friends!

Bless You Acquaintances!

Bless You Enemies!

Bless You Family!

Bless You Church!

Bless You Minister!

Bless You Ministry!

Bless You Angels!

Bless You Armor Bearer!

Bless You Bishop!

Bless You Elder!

Bless You Five—Fold Ministry!

Bless You Apostle!

Bless You Prophet!

Bless You Evangelist!

Bless You Teacher!

Bless You Pastor!

Bless You Governments (Church)

Bless You Ministry Of Helps!

Bless You College!

Bless You University!

Bless You Primary School!

Bless You Elementary School!

Bless You Junior High School!

Bless You High School!

Bless You Teachers!

Bless You Professors!

Bless You Faculty And Staff!

Bless You Students!

Bless You Full Scholarship!

Bless You Education!

Bless You Diploma!

Bless You GED!

Bless you Associate's Degree!

Bless You Bachelor's Degree!

Bless You Master's Degree!

Bless You Doctorate Degree!

Bless You Food!

Bless You Health!

Bless You Strength!

Bless You Favor!

Bless You Love!

Bless You Joy!

Bless You Peace!

Bless You Revelation!

Bless You Word Of God!

Bless You Trafford
Publishing Company!

Bless You Publishing Consultant!

Bless You Marketing Consultant!

Bless You Book Sales!

Bless You Books!

Bless You Movie Deals!

Bless You Movie Producers!

Bless You Television Scripts!

Bless You Live Theater Performances!

Bless You Broadway!

Bless You Bookstore Preview Buyers!

Bless You Libraries!

Bless You Book Customers!

Bless You Substantial Royalties!

As you can see, there is no limit to what you can bless, whom you can bless, when you can bless, how you can bless, how long you can bless, where you can bless, or why you can bless!!!

The bottom line? Just bless everything and everybody around the clock, 24 hours a day, 7 days a week,

365 days a year, 366 days in leap year!!!

As you hear these words coming from us, your parents, take them to heart, and let them saturate the Spirit in you that is fully developed until you get to earth, upon which you can further develop as you walk in the Spirit.

Everything you will ever need and all your heart will ever desire, dwells in, resides in, and abides in the Spirit! Walk in the Spirit daily to see all the money, love, happiness, prosperity, wealth, riches, joy, peace, promotions, raises, bonuses, perfect salary, career, houses, mansions, estates, cars, and happy marriage that belong exclusively and specifically to you.

Imagine that you are a Prince, Princess, King, or Queen who is sitting with Christ in heavenly places and that you are reigning with Christ on earth. See yourself being given the royal responsibility of spending the whole day blessing everything and everyone who comes into your immediate space and presence.

After the day ends, send these same individuals thoughts of blessings. Seeing yourself being a blessing . . . seeing yourself blessing . . . and seeing yourself being blessed as a result of blessing is the greatest thing on earth!!!

You Live In Christ!!!

My child, where you live, and how you live is important—to us and to God. You were not born to do any ole thing, any kind of way, and call it God. You have been called to be an Ambassador of Christ. You were born to live in a manner that glorifies God and the lifestyle he has mapped out for you.

According to 2 Corinthians 5:17, it says, "Therefore if any man be in Christ, he is a new creature: old things are past away; behold, all things are become new."

The whole point of today's discussion is that you learn what it means to live in Christ. For all practical and Spiritual purposes, you live in Christ in the same way people live within their chosen state.

Think of Christ as a state. When you think of living in Christ think of yourself as living in the State of Christ.

Perhaps you will notice that people frequently ask the question, "Where do you live?" "Where are you from?" Just say, "I live in Christ!!! I" live in the State of Christ!!!" "I am from Christ!!!" It will make all the difference in the world!!!

Living in Christ, in the State of Christ, is better than living in Beverly Hills, California, or the richest state or country in the world. It is the next best thing to living in Heaven as mentioned in Revelation 21. Living in Christ is the greatest place to live!!!

You Live In Christ Affirmations!!!

The Lord Is My Refuge
And My Fortress!!!

I Dwell In The Secret Place
Of The Most High!!!

The Lord Is My Dwelling Place!!!

I Dwell In Safety!!!

I Live In God!!!

I Live In The Omnipresence Of God!!!

I Live In The Omnipotence Of God!!!

I Live In Jehovah God!!!

I Live In Jehovah Rapha!!!

I Live In Jehovah Jireh!!!

I Live In Jehovah Shalom!!!

I Live In Christ!!!

I Dwell In Christ!!!

I Abide In Christ!!!

I Reside In Christ!!!

I Preside In Christ!!!

I Live In The Holy Ghost!!!

I Live In The Holy Spirit!!!

I Live In The Spirit On The Lord's Day!!!

I Live In The State Of Jehovah God!!!

I Live In the Sovereignty
Of Jehovah God!!!

I Live In The State Of Christ!!!

I Live In The State Capital Of Christ!!!

I Live In The Lordship of Jesus Christ!!!

I Live In the Jurisdiction Of Christ!!!

I Live In The Precinct Of Christ!!!

I Live In The District Of Christ!!!

I Live In The New Heaven
And The New Earth!!!

I Live In The New Jerusalem!!!

I Live In New Jerusalem!!!

I Live In The State Of
Unadulterated Thanksgiving!!!

I Live In the State Of
Unadulterated Praise!!!

I Live In The State Of
Unadulterated Worship!!!

Who You Are In Christ!!!

As your parents, *what we say to you NOW*, and for the rest of your life, *matters*. It is important for you to know who you are in Christ!

Who You Are In Christ Affirmations!!!

You Are Blessed!

You Are The Most Blessed Forever!

You Are Prosperous!

Whatever You Do Shall Prosper!

The Lord Delights In Your Prosperity!

You Are Very Rich!

You Are Very Wealthy!

Wealth and Riches Are In Your House!

You Are Very Successful!

You Are Privileged!

You Are Very Fortunate!

You Are Happily Married!

You Have A Great Future
Ahead Of You!

You Are A King (Males)!

You Are A Queen (Females)!

You Are A Prince (Males)!

You Are A Princess (Females)!

You Are Royalty!

I Reign With Christ For A Living!

Moreover, you should know that the Greatest Name on Earth Is Jesus! The Two Most Powerful Words On Earth Are, "I AM!

Whatever words you add to these two powerful words, "I Am," will be established in your life. So go ahead and say to yourself silently and out loud each day:

I Am Blessed!

I Am The Most Blessed Forever!

I Am A Blesser!

I Am Prosperous!

Whatever I Do Shall Prosper!

The Lord Delights In My Prosperity!

I Am Very Rich!

I Am Very Wealthy!

Wealth And Riches Are In My House!

I Am Very Successful!

I Am Privileged!

I Am Very Fortunate!

I Am Happily Married!

I Am A King (Males)!

I Am A Queen (Females)!

I Am A Prince (Males)!

I Am A Princess (Females)!

I Am Royalty!

I Reign With Christ For A Living!

I Have A Great Future Ahead Of Me!

What Christ Did!!!

My dearly beloved, you are redeemed from the curse of the law according to Galatians 3:13, which says, "Christ hath redeemed us from the curse of the law, being made a curse for us, for it is written, cursed is everyone who hangs on a tree, that the <u>blessing</u> <u>of Abraham</u> might come on the Gentiles through Jesus Christ, that we might receive the promise of the Spirit through faith."

What that means in laymen's terms is this: "Surely He hath borne our griefs, and carried our sorrows, yet we did esteem Him stricken, smitten of God, and afflicted. But He was wounded for our transgressions, He was bruised for our iniquities, the chastisement of our peace was upon Him, and by His stripes, we are healed (Isaiah 53:5-6)!!!

"Who His own self bare our sins in His own body on the tree, that we, being dead to sins, should live unto righteousness: by whose stripes ye were healed" (1 Peter 2:24)!!!

As long as you live on the face of the earth, and even into Eternity, it is highly valuable that you keep the birth, the death, the burial, the resurrection, and the ascension of Christ into Heaven, and even His second coming in mind at all times.

Here are just a few things you should know about why Christ was born and why He died on the cross for your sins. If you will take these things to heart, and meditate on them daily, your life on earth will be far greater than if you did not know why Christ came.

What Christ Did
Affirmations!!!

When Christ died on the cross for you over 2,000 years ago, Christ did the following:

Christ took your sicknesses and Gave you His Perfect Health!

Christ took your diseases and Gave you His Perfect Healing!

Christ took your poverty and Gave you His Riches in Glory!

Christ took your curses and Gave you His Blessings!

Christ took your debts and
Gave you His Debt Cancellation!

Christ took your broke spirit and
Gave you His Rich Spirit!

Christ took your lack and
Gave you His All Sufficiency!

Christ took your life and
Gave you His Abundant Life!

Christ took your shabby life and
Gave You His Eternal Life!

Christ took your nature and
Gave you His Righteous Nature!

Christ took your sins and
Gave you His Righteousness!

Christ took your past and
Gave you His Future!

Christ took your present and
Gave you His Perfect Gift!

Christ took your failures and
Gave you His Success!

Christ took your shame and
Gave you His Glory!

Christ took you dishonor and
Gave you His Honor!

Christ took your disgrace and
Gave you His Grace!

Christ took your favor and
Gave you His Unmerited Favor!

Christ took your pride and
Gave you His Dignity!

Christ took your low self-image and
Gave You His Self-Worth!

Christ took your brokenness and
Gave you His Wholeness!

Christ took your emptiness and
Gave you His Fullness of Joy!

Christ took your loneliness and
Gave you His Presence!

Christ took your disproval and
Gave you His Seal of Approval!

Christ took your disappointments and
Gave You His Appointment!

Christ took your weakness and
Gave you His Strenth!

Christ took your despair and
Gave you His Hope!

Christ took your powerlessness and
Gave you His Power!

Christ took your helplessness and
Gave you His Help!

Christ took your friendlessness and
Gave you His Friendship!

Christ took your humanity and
Gave you His Divinity!

Christ took your selfishness and
Gave you His Generosity!

Christ took your broken dreams and
Gave you His Vision!

Christ took your unhappiness and
Gave you His Happiness!

Christ took your displeasure and
Gave you His Pleasure!

Christ took your hell and
Gave you His Paradise!

Christ took your hell and
Gave you His Heaven!

Christ took your unfaithfulness and
Gave you His Faithfulness!

In short, my child, Christ took your place on the cross 2,000 years ago, so you can sit with Him in Heavenly Places today (Ephesians 2:6). Christ took your position on the cross so you could reign with Him on the earth.

You were born to reign with Christ on earth. The minute you are born again and accept Christ as your personal Lord and Savior, you have been born into the family of God—a family where both God and His Son, Jesus Christ, sit on the throne in Heaven and on the throne of your heart as the undisputable KING!!!

That makes you either a Prince or King, Princess or Queen, who has the right to Rule and Reign with Christ, as you live like Christ—ROYALLY!!!

Consider these words in Revelation 5:12: "Worthy is the Lamb that was slain to receive power, <u>and</u> riches, <u>and</u> wisdom, <u>and</u> strength, <u>and</u> honor <u>and</u> glory, <u>and</u> blessing." You, my son or daughter, are worthy to receive all these things on earth and more, even into Eternity in the New Heaven and the New Earth!!!

If you will commit yourself daily to <u>Living</u> like Christ, and <u>accepting</u> His Atoning Work (Redemptive, shed blood at Calvary,on Calvary, you will never Live beneath your privilege or higher than your privilege. You will live at your privilege, "far above all principality, and power, and might, and dominion, and every name that is named, not only in this world, but in the world to come" (Ephesians 1:21)!!!

In closing, I will not wish you the best of luck!!! Why??? You do not need luck; You are the most blessed forever because *What You Say To Your Child Really Does Matter!!!* And we chose, and will always choose to say only what Christ has said about you through His Written, Living, and Rhema Word!!!

We cannot wait for your arrival!!! Next to God, you are the most valuable person in our life. You are wanted!!! You are loved, and you are very highly thought of—forever!!!!!

God's Final Word!!!

My precious child, there is one final word that you must know without question—a word that will change the way you walk in the world as you go about your Heavenly Father's business.

The Bible (King James Version) declares these words found in Romans 6:12: "Let not sin reign in your mortal body, that ye should obey it in the lusts thereof."

For more clarification, the Amplified Bible puts it this way: "Let not sin therefore rule as king in your mortal bodies to make you yield to its cravings and be subject to its lusts and evil passions."

As we have already told you, your Heavenly Father is a King and He is The Most Sovereign. And His Kingdom shall have no end. His Son, Jesus Christ, is Lord of lords and King of kings, and you have been destined to reign with Christ upon the earth.

All that means is that the minute you accept Christ as your personal Savior, your reign sitting next to Christ begins. Again, all that means is that you will reign as a king or queen, prince or princess.

God's Final Word Affirmations!!!

Every day, you should say the following to enforce your reign:

The Sovereignty Of God Reigns In My Mortal Body!

The Majesty Of God Reigns In My Mortal Body!

The Shekinah Glory Of God Reigns In My Mortal Body!

The Riches Of God's Glory Reigns In My Mortal Body!

The Lordship Of Jesus Christ Reigns In My Mortal Body!

The Divinity Of Christ Reigns
In My Mortal Body!

The Blood Of The Lamb
Reigns In My Mortal Body!

The Lamb Of God Reigns
In My Mortal Body!

The Second Adam Reigns
In My Mortal Body!!!

The Baptism Of The Holy Ghost
Reigns In My Mortal Body!

The Baptism In The Holy Ghost
Reigns In My Mortal Body!

The Kingdom Of God Reigns
In My Mortal Body!

The Kingdom Of Heaven
Reigns In My Mortal Body!

Heaven Reigns In My Mortal Body!

Heaven On Earth Reigns
In My Mortal Body!

Paradise Reigns In My Mortal Body!

Perfect Health Reigns In
My Mortal Body!

Wealth And Riches Reign
In My Mortal Body!

The Marriage Of the Lamb
Reigns In My Mortal Body!

The New Heaven And The New
Earth Reigns In My Mortal Body!

Post Script!!!

I hope you are as delighted as I am about the possibilities that lie ahead for both you and your child. What you teach your child today, beginning in the womb, and after, even throughout his or her life, will significantly impact the Global Economy, and greatly affect future generations!!!

It is my sincere prayer that you will take each word in *What You Say To Your Child Really Does Matter* to heart, and imagine that each nurturing word is shaping your child's destiny, and charting out a dynamic course for him or her that is second to none!!!

In times such as these, it is imperative that both you and your child know that God's greatest desire is to empower your child to receive that which no one in any time in history has ever seen, heard or imagined!!!

Both you and your beloved child are on the cutting edge of the greatest life and journey on earth, to walk where others coming before have dared not tread!!!

Seize the moment and empower your child to step outside the mundane and mediocre to gloriously step into the *more excellent*!!! *What You Say To Your Child Really Does Matter!!!*

Everyday, make these words a part of you and your child's daily confessions and affirmations and note the difference in his or her life versus life had you not chosen to declare these words:

Satan Is Defeated!!!

Satan Has Been Cast Into
The Lake Of Fire!!!

God Is Sovereign!!!

God Is Supreme!!!

God Is On The Throne!!!

The Lord Is In His Holy Temple!!!

Jesus Christ Is Lord!!!

Jesus Christ Is The Head
Of The Church!!!

Jesus Christ Is The Head
Of My House!!!

Christ Reigns!!!

The Holy Ghost Is In Office!!!

The Holy Ghost Is In Session!!!

The Holy Ghost Is In Class!!!

The Holy Ghost Is In Power!!!

Bibliography

- Anatomy Answers. (n.d.). What are the stages of postnatal development? *In Anatomy Q & A.* Retrieved January 10, 2013, from Answers.com Web site: http://www.answers.com/topic/what-are-the-stages-of-postnatal-development
- *Thesaurus.com: Nurturing.* (2013). Retrieved from http://thesaurus.com/browse/nurturing?__utma=1.1294768603.1357938470.1357938470.1357938470.1&__utmb=1.6.8.1357938506475&__utmc=1&__utmx=-&__utmz=1.1357938470.1.1.utmcsr=(direct)|utmccn=(direct)|utmcmd=(none)&__utmv=-&__utmk=213244948